SOLVE IT! MATH IN SPACE

MATH ON
JUPITER

By Barbara M. Linde

Gareth Stevens
PUBLISHING

Please visit our website, www.garethstevens.com. For a free color catalog of all our high-quality books, call toll free 1-800-542-2595 or fax 1-877-542-2596.

Library of Congress Cataloging-in-Publication Data

Names: Linde, Barbara M., author.
Title: Math on Jupiter / Barbara M. Linde.
Description: New York : Gareth Stevens Publishing, [2017] | Series: Solve it!
  Math in space | Includes index.
Identifiers: LCCN 2015045742 | ISBN 9781482449389 (pbk.) | ISBN 9781482449327 (library bound) | ISBN
9781482449228 (6 pack)
Subjects: LCSH: Jupiter (Planet)–Juvenile literature. | Jupiter
  (Planet)–Exploration–Juvenile literature.
Classification: LCC QB661 .L584 2017 | DDC 523.45–dc23
LC record available at http://lccn.loc.gov/2015045742

First Edition

Published in 2017 by
Gareth Stevens Publishing
111 East 14th Street, Suite 349
New York, NY 10003

Copyright © 2017 Gareth Stevens Publishing

Designer: Laura Bowen
Editor: Therese Shea

Photo credits: Cover, p. 1 (Jupiter) ModeList/Shutterstock.com; cover, p. 1 (metal banner) Eky Studio/Shutterstock.com; cover, pp. 1–24 (striped banner) M. Stasy/Shutterstock.com; cover, pp. 1–24 (stars) angelinast/Shutterstock.com; cover, pp. 1–24 (math pattern) Marina Sun/Shutterstock.com; pp. 4–24 (text box) Paper Street Design/Shutterstock.com; pp. 5 (main), 9, 11 (moons), 13 (all), 15, 17 (main), 19 (all), 21 (main) courtesy of NASA.com; p. 5 (inset) MarcelClemens/Shutterstock.com; p. 7 Alhovik/Shutterstock.com; p. 11 (Galileo) Justus Sustermans/Wikimedia Commons; p. 17 (inset) Jcpag2012/Wikimedia Commons; p. 21 (inset) Ely1/Wikimedia Commons.

Printed in the United States of America

CPSIA compliance information: Batch #CS16GS: For further information contact Gareth Stevens, New York, New York at 1-800-542-2595.

CONTENTS

Words in the glossary appear in **bold** type the first time they are used in the text.

MISSION TO JUPITER

Do you love looking up at the night sky? If you do, chances are you've seen Jupiter. It's so big and bright that you can spot it without a **telescope**. The ancient Greeks and Romans noticed Jupiter, too. They named the planet after the king of their gods. Today, we still use the Roman name, Jupiter.

How do we know things about Jupiter? Robotic spacecraft explore it and send back important **data**. In this book, you'll visit the largest planet in the **solar system**. Start your countdown now!

YOUR MISSION

Scientists who study space and the objects in it use math. As you read this book, you'll be the scientist. Get ready to use your math skills as you complete the **missions**. Look for the upside-down answers to check your work. Good luck!

The Hubble Space Telescope took this image of Jupiter.

Hubble Space Telescope

WHERE IS JUPITER?

Jupiter is the fifth planet from the sun, between Mars and Saturn. It's about 483,680,000 miles (778,410,000 km) from the sun. Jupiter's **orbit** takes 4,330 Earth days, which is almost 12 Earth years! Jupiter rotates, or turns, more quickly than any other planet. A full rotation takes about 10 hours.

YOUR MISSION

The time it takes a planet to make a full rotation is called its day. An Earth day is about 24 hours long. Jupiter's day is about 10 hours long. About how much longer is an Earth day?

$$24 - 10 = ?$$

The planets, in order from the sun, are Mercury, Venus, Earth, Mars, Jupiter, Saturn, Uranus, and Neptune.

ANSWER: An Earth day is about 14 hours longer than a day on Jupiter.

A GAS GIANT

Jupiter is called a gas giant because it doesn't have a solid surface like Earth. You couldn't walk there or land a spacecraft. Instead, Jupiter's "surface" is clouds of hydrogen, helium, ammonia, and other gases. These gases are also in its poisonous **atmosphere**. The weather gets superhot and supercold.

YOUR MISSION

There are 4 terrestrial, or rocky, planets in our solar system: Mercury, Venus, Earth, and Mars. There are also 4 gas giants: Jupiter, Saturn, Uranus, and Neptune. How many planets are there total in our solar system?

$$4 + 4 = ?$$

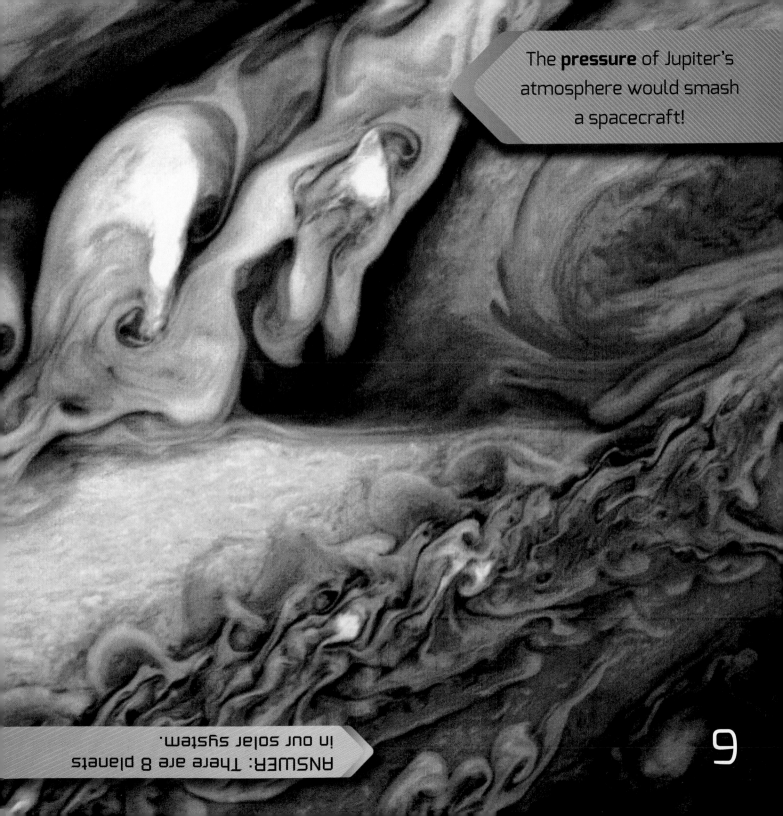

The **pressure** of Jupiter's atmosphere would smash a spacecraft!

ANSWER: There are 8 planets in our solar system.

9

GALILEO STUDIES JUPITER

Italian Galileo Galilei was the first person to use a telescope to observe Jupiter. In 1610, he discovered Jupiter's 4 largest moons. Before this discovery, many people thought all heavenly bodies circled Earth. Galileo saw the moons circle Jupiter. He helped prove the planets circle the sun.

YOUR MISSION

Galileo discovered the 4 largest moons. They're known now as the Galilean **satellites**. Jupiter has a total of 67 moons that we know of. How many moons were discovered by other astronomers?

$$67 - 4 = ?$$

Galileo

The moons Galileo observed are called Io (EYE-oh), Europa (yuu-ROH-puh), Ganymede (GAA-nih-meed), and Callisto (kuh-LIH-stoh).

Io

Europa

Ganymede

Callisto

ANSWER: Other astronomers discovered 63 more moons.

THE GALILEAN SATELLITES

Read this chart to find out more about the Galilean satellites.

	IO	EUROPA	GANYMEDE	CALLISTO
surface	sulfur	water ice	water ice, rock	water ice, rock
core	iron	iron	iron	ice, rock
diameter	2,256 miles (3,631 km)	1,945 miles (3,130 km)	3,273 miles (5,267 km)	2,986 miles (4,806 km)
average distance from Jupiter	262,200 miles (422,000 km)	417,000 miles (671,000 km)	665,000 miles (1,070,000 km)	1,170,000 miles (1,883,000 km)

Callisto

Europa

Ganymede

Io

NASA (National Aeronautics and Space Administration) spacecraft took these images of the surfaces of the Galilean satellites.

YOUR MISSION

How many of the Galilean satellites have water ice on their surfaces? How many of them have an iron core, or center? Show your answers as fractions. Use the chart to help you.

$$\frac{\text{satellites with water ice}}{\text{satellites}} = \frac{?}{?}$$

$$\frac{\text{satellites with iron core}}{\text{satellites}} = \frac{?}{?}$$

ANSWER: Water ice is on the surface of 3/4 of the Galilean satellites, and 3/4 of the Galilean satellites have iron cores.

JUPITER'S RINGS

Jupiter has rings! NASA's *Voyager 1* spacecraft discovered them in 1979. When **meteorites** crash into the moons, they create dust. This dust goes into orbit and forms the rings. The outer ring (actually a pair called the gossamer rings) is faint. The main ring is the brightest. The inner ring, called the halo, is thick.

YOUR MISSION

The 4 largest planets in our solar system have ring systems. According to NASA, Jupiter has 3 rings, Saturn has 7 rings, Neptune has 6 rings, and Uranus has 11 rings. Find out how many rings these planets have in all.

$$3 + 7 + 6 + 11 = ?$$

Here is a cutaway image of Jupiter's rings. Can you find the small moons that help create them?

gossamer rings

main ring

halo

Amalthea

Adrastea

Metis

Thebe

THE GREAT RED SPOT

Do you see the huge red spot in the photo of Jupiter? It's a storm made up of spinning clouds. It's like a **hurricane** on Earth, but much larger. In fact, this superhuge storm is as wide as 2 Earths! The Great Red Spot, as it's called, has been getting smaller. Scientists aren't sure yet why that's happening.

YOUR MISSION

The Great Red Spot is shrinking by about 580 miles each year. About how many miles will it shrink in 2 years?

$$580 \times 2 = ?$$

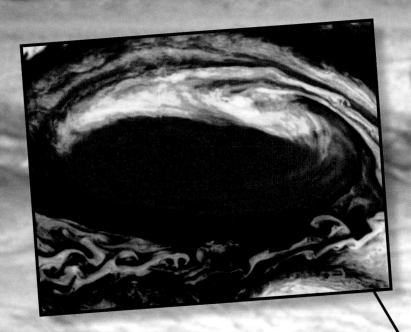

Scientists are also trying to learn why the Great Red Spot is red.

ANSWER: It will shrink about 1,160 miles (1,866 km) in 2 years.

NASA MISSIONS TO JUPITER

Jupiter is too far away to send manned, or crewed, missions to explore it. However, NASA has been sending robotic spacecraft to Jupiter since 1972. These missions often last for many years. The timeline on page 19 shows when each craft arrived at Jupiter and the kind of data recorded.

YOUR MISSION

The *Galileo* spacecraft was **launched** in 1989. It began to record data 6 years later. It crashed into Jupiter in 2003. About how long did it record data before it crashed?

$$1989 + 6 = x$$
$$2003 - x = ?$$

EXPLORING JUPITER

- 1973 *Pioneer 10* records images of Jupiter.

- 1974 *Pioneer 11* records images of Jupiter and the Great Red Spot.

- 1979 *Voyager 1* records images of Jupiter's moons.

- 1979 *Voyager 2* records data about the Great Red Spot and Io's volcanoes.

- 1992 *Ulysses* records data about Jupiter's **magnetic field**.

- 1995 *Galileo* records data about Jupiter's satellites, atmosphere, and **temperature**.

- 2000 *Cassini-Huygens* records thousands of images of Jupiter.

- 2007 *New Horizons* records measurements of Jupiter's moons' orbits.

Pioneer 10 and its images

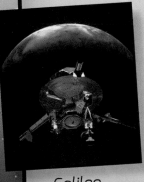

Voyager 1

Galileo

Pioneer 11

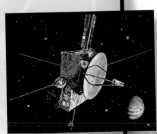

Ulysses

Cassini-Huygens launch

ANSWER: *Galileo* recorded data for about 8 years before it crashed.

NASA'S *JUNO* MISSION

Launched in 2011, the *Juno* spacecraft is expected to orbit Jupiter's north and south poles more than 30 times. It will burn up in Jupiter's atmosphere by 2018. Hopefully, *Juno* will help us answer many remaining questions about Jupiter's core, magnetic field, and more.

There's still so much to learn about Jupiter. Perhaps your next mission will take you there!

YOUR MISSION

Juno launched in 2011. Its path was corrected 1 year later. It received a speed boost by flying past Earth 1 year after that. It was set on course to arrive at Jupiter 3 years after that. About how many years was *Juno*'s journey to Jupiter? What year did it arrive?

$$1 + 1 + 3 = x \qquad 2011 + x = ?$$

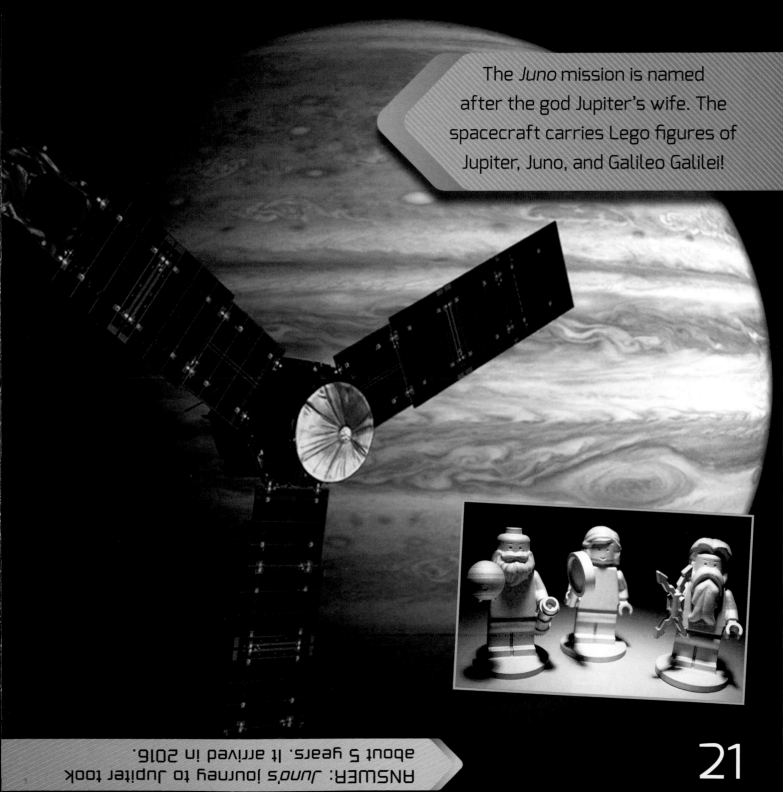

The *Juno* mission is named after the god Jupiter's wife. The spacecraft carries Lego figures of Jupiter, Juno, and Galileo Galilei!

ANSWER: *Juno's* journey to Jupiter took about 5 years. It arrived in 2016.

21

GLOSSARY

atmosphere: the mixture of gases that surround a planet

data: facts and figures

diameter: the distance from one side of a round object to another through its center

hurricane: a powerful storm that forms over water and causes heavy rainfall and high winds

launch: to send out with great force

magnetic field: the area around a magnet where its pull is felt

meteorite: a piece from a space rock that falls to a planet's or moon's surface

mission: a task or job a group must perform

orbit: to travel in a circle or oval around something, or the path used to make that trip

pressure: a force that pushes on something else

satellite: a space object that circles a larger object

solar system: the sun and all the space objects that orbit it, including the planets and their moons

telescope: a tool that makes faraway objects look bigger and closer

temperature: how hot or cold something is

FOR MORE INFORMATION

Books

Cunningham, Greg P. *Journey to Jupiter*. New York, NY: PowerKids Press, 2015.

Squire, Ann O. *Planet Jupiter*. New York, NY: Children's Press, 2014.

Taylor-Butler, Christine. *Jupiter*. New York, NY: Children's Press, 2008.

Websites

Mission to Jupiter!
spaceplace.nasa.gov/junoquest/en/
Play "JunoQuest" online.

What Is Jupiter?
www.nasa.gov/audience/forstudents/k-4/stories/nasa-knows/ what is jupiter-k4.html
Look at images of Jupiter taken from NASA spacecraft, and find out more about the gas giant.

INDEX